Jewish Values in Exodus:

If I Could Ask Miriam

Lesson Plan Manual

By Rachael Gelfman Schultz

BEHRMAN HOUSE

Behrman House, Inc.

www.behrmanhouse.com/values-bible

Library of Congress Cataloging-in-Publication Data

Names: Schultz, Rachael Gelfman, author.
Title: Jewish values in Exodus : if I could ask Miriam : lesson plan manual / by Rachael Gelfman Schultz.
Description: Springfield, NJ : Behrman House, [2016] | ?2016
Identifiers: LCCN 2015042255 | ISBN 9780874419283
Subjects: LCSH: Bible. Exodus--Study and teaching (Elementary) | Jewish ethics--Study and teaching (Elementary) | Jewish religious education--Teaching methods.
Classification: LCC BS1245.55 .S382 2016 | DDC 296.6/8083--dc23 LC record available at http://lccn.loc.gov/2015042255

Springfield, NJ 07081
www.behrmanhouse.com

ISBN 978-0-87441-928-3
Printed in the United States of America

Visit www.behrmanhouse.com/values-bible for more resources.

Contents

Introduction **5**

Structure of the Course 5

Using This Lesson Plan Manual 6

Teaching Strategies and Tips 6

Course Website 10

Introductory Lesson on Community **11**

Chapter 1: How Do I Find Courage? *The Midwives in Egypt* (*G'vurah*: Courage)

Lesson 1 13

Lesson 2 16

Chapter 2: What Makes a Good Leader? *Moses at the Burning Bush* (*Manhigut*: Leadership)

Lesson 1 18

Lesson 2 20

Chapter 3: How Can I Fight for Justice? *Moses Confronts Pharaoh* (*Tzedek*: Justice)

Lesson 1 22

Lesson 2 24

Chapter 4: What Am I Thankful For? *Song of the Sea* (*Hodayah*: Thankfulness)

Lesson 1 26

Lesson 2 28

Chapter 5: What Am I Committed To? *Receiving the Torah* (*Brit*: Covenant and Commitment)

Lesson 1 31

Lesson 2 34

Chapter 6: How Can I Learn to Forgive? *The Golden Calf* (*S'lichah*: Forgiveness)

Lesson 1 36

Lesson 2 38

Chapter 7: What Can I Give? *Building the Tabernacle* (*N'tinah*: Giving)

Lesson 1 40

Lesson 2 42

My Community Project **44**

Glossary **46**

Introduction

How can the Torah help us build strong communities and make our own unique contributions to those communities? *Jewish Values in Exodus: If I Could Ask Miriam* invites students to learn timeless Jewish community values through the stories of the Torah. With this course, students gain knowledge and understanding of biblical stories while exploring the connections between these stories and their lives. This course enriches students' Jewish identities by helping them view themselves as part of the Jewish people and its history. It also gives students opportunities to apply Jewish values in their everyday lives and communities.

STRUCTURE OF THE COURSE

Each chapter of *Jewish Values in Exodus: If I Could Ask Miriam* focuses on one story from Exodus and one Jewish value or *midah* (character trait) that we can learn from that story. The stories are introduced in the order they appear in the book of Exodus.

Jewish Values in Exodus: If I Could Ask Miriam is a unique book designed as a student-response journal, which includes creative, interactive activities that integrate Jewish texts with journal writing, drama, art, music, movement, and more. The Lesson Plan Manual presents fifteen ready-to-use lesson plans of fifty minutes each and includes suggestions for teaching all elements of the student-response journal.

Every chapter in the student-response journal includes the following features:

- **Telling the Story:** a creative exploration of the biblical story.
- **Digging Deeper:** questions that help students think more deeply about the biblical story.
- **Making Meaning:** an introduction to a Jewish value or concept—identified in both Hebrew and English—that is related to the biblical story.

Some chapters may also include:

- **Get on the Move:** a short movement-based activity related to the themes of the chapter.
- **Values in Action:** image-based examples of people whose example can be used to discuss the Jewish value that is the focus of the chapter.
- **What Would You Do?:** an exercise presenting real-life scenarios that call for applying the Jewish value that is the focus of the chapter.
- **Rabbis' Corner:** an exploration of a short rabbinic text that interprets the biblical story and/or the Jewish value that is the focus of the chapter.
- **Try This!:** experiential prompts for activities connecting Jewish values to students' lives.
- **Torah Timeline:** summaries of stories from Exodus (in the order they appear in the Bible) that relate to the theme of the chapter but are not covered in depth in this book; stories are presented with questions for further thought.
- **[The Jewish Value] and Me:** a journal-writing exercise to help students reflect on how the Jewish value covered in the chapter is relevant to their own lives.

USING THIS LESSON PLAN MANUAL

At the start of the year, map out when you plan to teach each chapter. Before starting a new chapter with your class, read through the Lesson Plan Manual to familiarize yourself with the chapter, and look at the biblical text to gain a deeper understanding of the story. You may choose to use the lessons exactly as they are, or you may decide to adapt them to fit the needs of your students. If you adapt the lessons, make sure to frame your lesson around central questions and goals. This manual makes frequent references to images and activities in the student-response journal and provides the corresponding page numbers for easy reference.

Each lesson plan in this manual includes the following sections:

- **Essential Question:** an overarching question that reflects the main idea of the lesson. You might write this question on the board before class begins and refer back to it at the end of class.
- **Goals:** specific goals for each lesson corresponding to the concepts and ideas that students should understand when they complete the lesson.
- **Lesson at a Glance:** a brief overview of the lesson, including a description of the Jewish value covered in the lesson and its connection to the biblical story studied in the chapter.
- **Materials Needed:** a list of any handouts, arts-and-crafts supplies, or other materials needed for the lesson.
- **Getting Started**: a set induction to get students thinking about the ideas they will examine in the lesson.
- **Activities:** detailed descriptions of each activity in the lesson and a suggested time frame for each one.
- **Wrapping It Up:** a short activity or discussion to review and reflect on the main ideas presented in the lesson.

Some lessons may also include the following sections:

- **Extension Activity:** an optional activity to enrich students' understanding of the biblical story and the Jewish value covered in the lesson.
- **Resources for the Teacher:** additional background information and resources to enrich your understanding of the texts, themes, and people discussed in the chapter. All website links mentioned in this manual are hyperlinked on the course website, www.behrmanhouse.com/values-bible.

TEACHING STRATEGIES AND TIPS

Journal Writing

Each chapter of *Jewish Values in Exodus: If I Could Ask Miriam* includes open-ended questions for students to think over and write about. Through writing in their journals, students are able to reflect on the relevance of Jewish values to their lives and are encouraged to ask: Why is this Jewish value important to me? How can I act on this value in my own life?

Whenever it is time for students to write in their journals, tell your class that their writing is private and that they will not be required to share what they write with other students. At some point, students may volunteer to share some of their journal entries with the class, but this should never be mandatory.

Asking Questions

This course will likely raise questions for many students about God, the Bible, Jewish beliefs and values, and some biblical characters. Make sure that your classroom provides a safe space for students to ask questions by insisting that all members of the classroom community—teachers and students—listen to one another with respect and sensitivity. The student journal provides opportunities throughout the course for students to ask questions. Encourage your class to take advantage of these opportunities and to feel comfortable asking questions at other times as well. Remind students that there are no foolish questions. Asking questions helps us learn even when we don't find answers. Explain also that asking questions about our values is a lifelong process, and our response to questions may change over time.

More Than One Right Answer

Throughout the student-response journal there are questions designed to help students think more deeply about the material. In many cases there is not one correct answer; rather, there are multiple interpretations of a text and a number of different ways to connect a Jewish value to our lives. The Lesson Plan Manual offers possible answers to the questions in the student-response journal so as to give the teacher some suggestions about the different directions to take the class. These answers appear in italics. Please keep in mind that the answers given in the manual are not the only correct answers, and encourage students to be creative and to explore a broad range of possibilities.

Close Reading

One of the skills students work on in this course is close reading of biblical text. The goal in teaching this skill is for students to learn how to go beyond a basic understanding of biblical text and examine what the specific language used in a particular biblical passage suggests about the text's meaning.

Activities that teach close reading require students to:

- Pay attention to which details the Bible includes and which it excludes, and to consider the meaning behind how the text is written.
- Cite verses to support their arguments.
- Look closely at difficult or ambiguous phrases and think about ways to interpret the words.

Students may find close reading of biblical text difficult, especially at first, so be sure to provide them with the necessary support. It may be helpful for you to model close reading by doing an example together with the class before they work independently or in small groups. Close reading may be a new skill for many students, and they will develop the skill gradually.

Project-based Learning (PBL)
With project-based learning, students use the knowledge and skills they learn in class to solve real-world problems. Working alone, with a partner, or in a group, students make or develop something concrete to demonstrate what they have learned. When a class learns about Jewish values using this method of learning, students gain a deeper understanding of how these values are relevant to their lives. Classes can create their own PBL experiences, such as organizing a tzedakah campaign or a community-building project, by using many of the ideas in *Jewish Values in Exodus: If I Could Ask Miriam*. For more information about exciting activities that use project-based learning, visit www.behrmanhouse.com/project-based-learning.

At the end of the Lesson Plan Manual, you will find directions for a final project called "My Community Project." For this project, students are asked to plan and implement a project to improve their school, synagogue, or local community. The project should apply one or more of the values they have learned about in the course. See page 44 of this manual for more details.

Glossary of Hebrew Terms
Jewish Values in Exodus: If I Could Ask Miriam teaches some key Hebrew terms. Students are taught the Hebrew term for each value they learn about, as well as other important Hebrew words that are scattered throughout the journal. In order to help you reinforce students' Hebrew vocabulary, a glossary is included in the back of this book containing all of the Hebrew terms that the students learn throughout the course. You can use this glossary to play games reinforcing vocabulary. For example, play a memory game where students match the Hebrew word to its English translation or a competition in which teams earn points by being the first to give the correct translation of a Hebrew word.

Being Inclusive
Children vary in their learning styles. Some learn best with a hands-on approach, while others do best with a visual or auditory approach. In general, teachers who present material in a number of different ways are able to reach many more children than teachers who present material in just one manner.

Teachers of children with special needs have extra challenges. There are a broad range of cognitive, physical, and behavioral disabilities that impact learning. It is always helpful for the education director to find out from parents what kinds of accommodations are made for a special-needs child in their secular school. Below are some suggestions for teaching this course to children with learning, perceptual, or attention problems.

- For students with attention- and auditory-processing problems, teach the class in small increments and present one instruction at a time. Ask the children to repeat instructions, making sure they have processed them.
- For children with attention problems, limit teaching segments to between ten and fifteen minutes, and allow for movement between activities.

- For children who have problems with attention and/or their visual figure-ground, mask parts of the page so that they can see only the section that is being worked on.
- For children with fine-motor and handwriting problems, limit the amount of writing, drawing, and cutting required. Prepare the difficult parts of a project in advance, and have students finish the task in class. This is a good way to engage a classroom *madrich* or *madrichah.* (*The* Madrichim *Manual* [Behrman House] is an excellent resource for learning how to engage *madrichim* appropriately.)

Remember, the relationships you develop with your students—and the relationships they build with one another—are as important as the material you teach. Try to always model patience and respect for all.

Interpersonal and Intrapersonal Learners

Some students learn best through interacting with others ("interpersonal" learners); some learn best independently ("intrapersonal" learners). With this in mind, the lesson plans in this book were written with suggestions for independent student work, as well as activities and discussions to be done with a partner, group, or whole class. In general, if the Lesson Plan Manual does not specify that students should work with a partner or in a group, you should plan for a class discussion.

Group Work

Many of the lessons in this manual include suggestions for group work. Whenever possible, plan ahead for how you want to form these groups. For some tasks you will want to group together students with a variety of talents and interests. For others, you may choose to put together students with similar skills. It is important to vary the composition of your groups.

Group work is most successful when every member of the group knows his or her responsibilities. To help make a group's task (or tasks) clear, prepare written instructions before class. Many of the lesson plans in this manual include such instructions. Consider creating index cards that describe the different possible jobs. These will vary according to the type of group work. Some possible jobs are:

- Recorder—records the group's suggestions or findings.
- Reporter—reports the group's work to the class.
- Illustrator—creates an illustration of the group's ideas to be presented to the class.
- Investigator—researches to discover information.
- Encourager—encourages group members to stay on task.
- Reader—reads information to the group.

Consider laminating the job-description index cards and distributing them each time you do group work.

Integrating Technology

Your students are growing up in a world in which technology is part of their daily lives at home and at school. There are an infinite number of ways for you to take advantage of the Internet and digital applications to reinforce concepts; deepen your students' understanding of the subject matter; share what has been learned with students' families; and add creativity, interactivity, and excitement to your lessons.

Note that the Behrman House Online Learning Center offers a platform for sharing information and collaborating on projects. You can find more information about the Online Learning Center here: http://www.behrmanhouse.com/olc/discover-the-online-learning-center.

In addition, see below for information about the *Jewish Values in Exodus: If I Could Ask Miriam* course website.

COURSE WEBSITE

The course website, **www.behrmanhouse.com/values-bible**, provides valuable resources, including links to videos and additional reference materials, which can help you enrich your students' learning experience and deepen their understanding of the biblical stories and values covered in each chapter.

Download the ***Jewish Values in Exodus*** **Expansion Pack of Game Cards** and play a version of Apples to Apples. Match values words with the Bible story situations that best teach us those values—or make your own funny combinations of matches. One player gets to be the judge and decide who wins!

For your convenience, all links to outside materials referenced in the Lesson Plan Manual are hyperlinked from the website. There is no need to retype a lengthy URL from a lesson plan. Simply visit the website and click on the links you need.

Introductory Lesson on Community

Essential Question: What does community mean to you?

Goals: In this lesson, students will:

1. Define the word *community* for themselves.
2. Identify different communities in their lives.
3. Choose community values that are important to them.

Lesson at a Glance

This book explores values that are central to building community. Before beginning to learn about these values, it is helpful for students to take a step back and think about what community means to them in the larger sense of the word. In this introductory lesson, students make creative abstract models of an ideal community as a way to begin thinking about relationships and values within a community.

Materials Needed

- Modeling clay
- Popsicle sticks, toothpicks, pipe cleaners, glue, tissue paper, etc. (optional)

Activities

1. **Getting Started: Defining Community** (10 minutes)

Begin the class by saying that this course explores Jewish values that are related to the concept of community. Explain that before beginning the course, it is important to think about what we mean when we talk about community.

Students should respond to the first prompt on page 6 of their journals individually. Ask for volunteers to share their answers, and discuss the responses as a class. Make sure to address the following questions: Who is part of a community? What is a community member's relationship to the others in the community? What brings different members of a community together?

For example, one definition of community could be: *a group of people that share certain values or goals.*

2. **Community in My Life** (10 minutes)

Students respond to the second and third prompts on page 6 individually. When they are done, they can share what they have written with a classmate.

3. **Try This!** (15 minutes)

Following the instructions on page 6 of their journals, students use the provided materials to create models of an ideal community. Models should reflect the relationship between the different kinds of people in a community. For example, one student's model may be multicolored balls of the same size arranged in a circle and connected by toothpicks, while another student's model may be pieces of different colors of clay mixed together to form a chaotic mix of colors.

4. **Wrapping It Up** (15 minutes)

When all the students have finished their projects, they should walk around the classroom and view each other's models. After they have finished looking at the different models, go around the room and discuss each one. Begin by asking a few students to explain how they interpret a specific model, and then have the student who made the model explain what he or she was trying to express.

To finish the lesson, point out that people understand the idea of community in many different ways and that these varied understandings can affect how the students will approach the questions that will come up in this course. Explain that these understandings may change and develop as the class learns from the biblical stories and from each other. Let students know that the classroom will be a safe space for them to express their thoughts and feelings regarding community and Jewish values.

CHAPTER ❶

How Do I Find Courage? *The Midwives in Egypt*

Lesson 1

Essential Question: How can the biblical story of the midwives in Egypt inspire us to act courageously in our own lives?

Goals: In this lesson, students will:

1. Analyze the biblical story of the midwives Shifrah and Puah.
2. Learn the word *g'vurah* (courage) and explain how Shifrah and Puah demonstrated this trait.
3. Discuss how acting courageously can help us improve ourselves and create better communities.

Lesson at a Glance

The first chapter of the Book of Exodus tells the story of how the midwives Shifrah and Puah acted courageously to save the Hebrew baby boys and, as a result, ensure the survival of the Jewish people. In this lesson, students look closely at this biblical story to find out what gave the midwives the courage to do what they did and how their actions shaped Jewish history. Students use improvisation and trust games to explore what gives us courage and how courage can shape our lives as individuals and as a people.

Activities

1. Getting Started: Get on the Move (10 minutes)

Clear a large open area in your classroom for this exercise (journal page 7), and divide the students into pairs. Ask one pair to demonstrate how to do the exercise safely, according to the instructions in the student-response journal. Then have all pairs do the trust falls. During this activity, walk around the room to make sure that each pair is following the directions carefully and safely.

When all pairs have completed the exercise, students answer the questions on page 7 of their journals. Those who wish to can share their answers with the class.

Discuss: Would I have allowed myself to fall if I had not trusted my partner? How did my trust in my partner give me courage to fall?

2. Telling the Story (15 minutes)

Ask students to read the story on page 8 of their journals to themselves, or have one student read the story out loud. Then divide students into pairs (if you wish, you can use the same pairs as in the first activity) and have them do the two improvisational exercises, also on page 8, with their partners. Once everyone has completed the exercise, ask two pairs to act out both scenarios for the class, making sure they address the questions about the exercise in the student-response journal.

Discuss: What would you have done in Shifrah and Puah's situation? Why?

3. **Digging Deeper** (15 minutes)

Ask students to look back at the text on page 8 and raise any questions they have about the story. Then discuss the questions on page 9 as a class.

For the second question, ask students to find a verse that supports their answer and to read it out loud to the class. Note that in this course, you will work with the students on the skill of close reading. One of the ways to teach this skill is to ask students to cite biblical quotes that support their opinions.

Possible answers to these questions include:

1) *The midwives risked their lives to save the Hebrew babies. They also risked their livelihoods and their reputations.*
2) *The midwives' fear of God gave them the courage to defy Pharaoh and save the babies. This answer is supported by the verse: "But the midwives feared God, and they did not do as the king of Egypt had ordered them."*
3) *Perhaps being together helped give Shifrah and Puah the courage to defy Pharaoh. They could support one another in making a risky decision and following through with it.*

Following up on the third question, ask students: Can being part of a community give us courage, just as Shifrah and Puah may have gained courage from being together? If so, how?

Tell the class to think about when they did the trust falls and how their trust in one another gave them and their partners the courage to fall backward, how in general, trust in others can help give us courage.

Some other questions that may come up during the textual study are: Why do you think God "made houses" for Shifrah and Puah? Does the text mean that God literally made houses? What else could it mean? How is making houses for the midwives an appropriate reward for what they did?

Point out that "houses" may not mean literal houses, but, rather, families. God rewarded the midwives, who saved other people's babies, by giving them families of their own (some commentaries say they were previously infertile), or, according to another interpretation, they were rewarded by being given families who became Levites, part of the priestly class. Some commentaries say that Shifrah was Yocheved, Moses's mother, and Puah was Miriam, Moses's sister, or Elisheva, Aaron's wife.

4. **Wrapping It Up: Making Meaning** (10 minutes)

Write the word *g'vurah* (גבורה) on the board in Hebrew and define it as a class. Discuss: What is courage?

Students should answer the questions on page 10 of their journals individually and then discuss their answers in small groups.

Extension Activity

TRY THIS! (PAGE 13): Have students prepare questions to ask a family member (as described on page 13), and then have them interview this family member at home. Students can share their stories and pictures in the next class.

Resources for the Teacher

See the course website at www.behrmanhouse.com/values-bible for:

- Commentaries, *midrashim*, and other background information regarding Shifrah and Puah. One interesting question raised in this reference material is whether Shifrah and Puah were Jewish or Egyptian. Students may ask this question as well. If this topic comes up, discuss whether seeing the midwives as being Jewish or Egyptian affects our understanding of the story and the midwives' choices.
- More information on Jewish midwives throughout history. Read the stories of famous Jewish midwives and explore their important role in Jewish history.

Chapter ❶ / Lesson 2

Essential Question: How can courage help build community?

Goals: In this lesson, students will:

1. Discuss what helps us act courageously and what makes it difficult for us to do so.
2. Identify the Israelite women's acts of courage in the Exodus story.
3. Explore ways that they can contribute to their own communities through acts of courage.

Lesson at a Glance

The midwives were the first of a series of women who acted courageously to save the Israelites in Egypt. In this lesson, students learn about these women and how their courageous acts ensured that the Jewish people survived as a nation. Students also explore how these women can inspire us to be courageous in our own lives and contribute to our communities.

Activities

1. Getting Started: What Would You Do? (15 minutes)

Ask for volunteers to act out the scenario on page 11 of the student journal, with different students acting as Jake, his two friends, Ethan, the onlooker, and the onlooker's two friends. Have the students show a number of ways the situation could unfold by acting out different choices Ethan could make and how the others would respond to him. You can switch actors, allowing for different students to act out the different possible outcomes.

Students then complete the sentences on page 11 on their own. When they are finished, they can share their answers in pairs.

2. My Community Project (5 minutes)

Introduce the community project that is explained on page 11 of the student journal. Explain that at the end of the course, each student will be required to organize a community project that involves using one or more of the values they studied in the course. Tell students that as they go through each chapter, they should think about what community project they might want to do that could involve applying the value they are studying.

Ask: What project could you do that would require applying the value of courage?

One example might be an anti-bullying project.

3. Torah Timeline (15 minutes)

Have students read the text on page 12 of their journals to themselves. Next, ask one student to read the text out loud, and instruct the rest of the class to stand up any time the reader gets to an act of courage. Each time one or more students stands up, ask one of the standing students to explain why he or she thinks this is an act of courage.

Students then answer the questions on page 12 in small groups. Go from group to group, asking questions and providing help. Point out that these stories describe the very early years of the nation. Explain that in Genesis, before the Book of Exodus, the Hebrews are described as a family, yet by the time the Hebrews left Egypt and arrived at Mount Sinai, they were a nation. The midwives literally helped to ensure the survival of the nation, but all the women were midwives in a figurative sense—because their acts of courage enabled the continuation of the Jewish people.

Examples of acts of courage that help to build community could include situations from student life in school, such as standing up for someone who is being teased or saying no to cigarettes, alcohol, or drugs. They may also include examples from modern history, like soldiers who fight terrorists or politicians who stand up for values that may be unpopular.

4. Wrapping It Up: *G'vurah and Me* (15 minutes)

Students answer the questions on page 13 of their journals individually and then share what they wrote with another student. Students should then write one of the "I can" statements from their journals on a long slip of paper (without their names) and hand them in. You should then paste all the pieces of paper on a board in the classroom.

Extension Activity

ANTI-BULLYING VIDEO FROM ISRAEL: Watch the video on the course website, www.behrmanhouse.com/values-bible, as a class. Before watching the video, give students the background information to the video based on the article on the course website.
Discuss: What risks did George Amira take in making this video? What do you think gave him the courage to make it? What impact do you think the video has on viewers?

Chapter 2

What Makes a Good Leader?

Moses at the Burning Bush

Lesson 1

Essential Question: How can the story of Moses inspire us to take on leadership in our own lives?

Goals: In this lesson, students will:

1. Analyze the story of Moses at the burning bush.
2. Define the term *manhigut* (leadership) and explain how Moses gained the confidence to lead.
3. Discuss how to decide what is a good time to take on a leadership role and when is the right time to step back and not take on leadership responsibilities.

Lesson at a Glance

When God called to Moses at the burning bush and told him that he would lead the Israelites out of Egypt, Moses was reluctant to take on leadership. In this lesson, students look at how Moses gained the confidence to become perhaps the greatest leader of the Jewish people. Through Moses's story, students explore questions of how, when, and why to take on leadership roles.

Activities

1. Getting Started: Get on the Move (10 minutes)

Clear an open space in the classroom for students to sit in a circle and play the game described on page 14 of their journals. At the end of the game, students answer the questions on page 14 individually. When they are finished, they can share some of their answers with the group. Explain that in this lesson the class will discuss why one person might want to take on a leadership position while another might be reluctant to do so. Reflect back to the class some of the reasons they identify for wanting, and not wanting, to take on leadership.

2. Telling the Story (15 minutes)

Ask three students to read the story on pages 15–16 out loud, with each reading a different part (the narrator, Moses, or God). When they are done reading the story, ask the students to underline all of the verses in which Moses shows reluctance to take on leadership. They should do this on their own.

Ask: How many of Moses's responses did you underline?

Students then compare their underlined verses with a partner.

3. **Digging Deeper** (10 minutes)

Ask students to answer the first two questions on page 17 of their journals in pairs. Then discuss the third question as a class. Here are possible answers to the questions:

1) *Responses of Moses that indicate his reluctance to become a leader include:*
    - *"Who am I that I should go to Pharaoh and free the children of Israel from Egypt?"*
    - *"But they will not believe me and will not listen to me, for they will say: 'God has not appeared to you.'"*
    - *"Please, God, I am not a man of words, neither in the past nor now that You have spoken to Your servant. I am slow of speech and slow of tongue."*
    - *"Please, God, make someone else your messenger."*
2) *Moses's reluctance seems to stem from his lack of confidence in himself as a leader and in his ability to convince the people of Israel to follow him.*
3) *Responses of God that help Moses gain the confidence to become a leader include:*
    - *"I will be with you. This will be a sign that I am with you: When you have freed the people from Egypt, you will worship God on this mountain."*
    - *"You should say to the Israelites: 'The Lord, the God of your ancestors, the God of Abraham, the God of Isaac, and the God of Jacob, has sent me to you.' "*
    - *God gives Moses three signs that God has sent him.*
    - *"Who gives people speech? Who makes people mute or deaf, seeing or blind? Is it not I, God? Now go, and I will be with you as you speak and teach you what to say."*
    - *"Is there not your brother Aaron the Levite? I know that he can speak well. . . He will serve as your spokesman."*

    God gives Moses confidence by telling him that he is not alone; God will support him as a leader; and Moses's brother will speak for him. Support from others is crucial for successful leadership.
4) *Perhaps the Torah tells us about Moses's doubts and lack of confidence to show that leaders are not always confident in themselves and their ability to lead. They, too, have doubts. We should know that even if we doubt ourselves, we can still become leaders and overcome our doubts.*

Point out that in general, our biblical leaders are not portrayed in the Bible as perfect. Ask the class: Does this change the way we relate to biblical leaders or what we can learn from them?

4. **Wrapping It Up: Making Meaning** (15 minutes)

Write on the board "*Being a leader means . . .* " Ask students to complete the sentence by writing their responses on the board. Students then complete the exercise on journal page 18 on their own.

If time permits, divide the class into small groups. Have some groups act out a situation in which it is good for a person to take on leadership; others act out a situation when it is better to step back and not take on a leadership role; and other groups act out a situation that might occur in a community without a leader. The skits should be about scenarios that could happen in the students' everyday lives.

Chapter ❷ / Lesson 2

Essential Question: What makes a good leader?

Goals: In this lesson, students will:

1. Identify qualities of a good leader.
2. Research leaders in the Bible, Jewish history, and today.
3. Discuss how they can take on more leadership roles in their own lives, what the challenges of leadership are, and how these challenges can be overcome.

Lesson at a Glance

Students learn about famous Jews in the Bible, Jewish history, and today to determine what does (or does not) make these people good leaders. At the end of the lesson, students reflect on how they can be good leaders in their own lives.

Materials Needed

- Poster board and markers
- Device with Internet access for each pair
- Printouts of short biographies of each person featured in the Values in Action exercise, if Internet is not available to students. (See Resources for the Teacher at the end of this lesson.)

Activities

1. Getting Started: Values in Action (10 minutes)

With a partner, students choose one of the famous Jewish people from the exercise on pages 20–21 of the journal and discuss whether or not that person is a good leader. Have one student in the pair argue why the person is a good leader and the other argue why the person is not a good leader. If there is time, and students have access to the Internet, they can learn more about that person online. If there is no Internet access in the classroom, give the students some printouts (that you prepared in advance) describing these people's lives (see Resources for the Teacher at the end of this lesson).

Discuss as a class: What questions about leadership came up during this exercise? For those you thought were good leaders, what made them good? For those you thought were not good leaders, why not?

Some other questions to discuss: Is someone a good leader just because he or she is a celebrity? What is the relationship between fame and leadership? Does being a philanthropist (giving a lot of money to charity) make a person a good leader? Must a good leader be a good role model?

2. Rabbis' Corner (10 minutes)

At the conclusion of your discussion about the people featured in Values in Action, have students brainstorm the qualities they think are important in a good leader, and ask them to write their answers on the top of page 19 in their journals. Write a list of leadership qualities on the board. Then discuss the second question on page 19 as a class.

Possible answers include:

- *Moses has compassion and a sense of justice, as we see when he stands up for the Israelite being beaten.*
- *Moses is humble, as we see in the story of the burning bush.*
- *Moses has a supportive family, as we see when his mother and sister go to great lengths to protect him as a baby and when his brother Aaron serves as his spokesperson.*
- *Because of his privileged upbringing in Pharaoh's palace, Moses has connections to people in power. He understands what it means to be powerful and how to relate to powerful people.*

Students then read the midrash on page 19 in pairs and answer the question that follows it. Walk around the room to make sure each pair understands the midrash.

One possible answer to the question is:

Moses shows compassion and mercy to the lamb, proving that he will be a good leader. Mercy and compassion are important qualities for leaders to possess, because if leaders have compassion for the people they lead, they will treat them well and not take advantage of their position of power.

3. **Election Campaign** (25 minutes)

In small groups, students do the exercise on page 21 of the journal. They can choose leaders from the Bible (such as one of the forefathers or foremothers, the midwives, Miriam, or Moses), a leader from Jewish history (such as Judah Maccabee, Theodor Herzl, Hannah Senesh, David Ben-Gurion, or Albert Einstein), or from current events (such as the people featured in Values in Action on pages 20–21). Once groups complete their posters, ask a representative from each group to present the poster to the class and explain why that person was a good leader. Take a vote on the best leader presented, with the condition that students cannot vote for the leader their group presented.

If possible, hang the posters in the classroom or in the hallway.

4. **Wrapping It Up: *Manhigut* and Me** (5 minutes)

Students complete this exercise (on journal page 22) individually. Have a few students share one way they would like to take on more leadership in their lives.

Resources for the Teacher

For more information on the people in the Values in Action exercise, visit the course website at www.behrmanhouse.com/values-bible.

Also visit the course website for more information on Midrash, more examples of Jewish leaders, and information about each one.

Chapter 3

How Can I Fight for Justice?

Moses Confronts Pharaoh

Lesson 1

Essential Question: How can the story of Moses confronting Pharaoh help us to fight for justice?

Goals: In this lesson, students will:

1. Analyze the story of Moses and Aaron confronting Pharaoh.
2. Define the term *tzedek* (justice) and explain how and why Moses and Aaron fought for justice.
3. Discuss how to identify injustice.

Lesson at a Glance

When Moses and Aaron confronted Pharaoh to demand that he let the people of Israel go, they provided a model for those fighting for justice throughout the ages. In this lesson, students take a closer look at the biblical story of Moses and Aaron confronting Pharaoh. Through movement, textual study, and personal reflection, students consider how we identify injustice and what motivates us to act in response to it.

Materials Needed

- Spoons, one per student
- Golf balls or eggs, one per student

Activities

1. Getting Started: Get on the Move (10 minutes)

Clear a large space in the classroom, and have an egg race according to the instructions on page 23 of the student journal. If necessary, go outside or to a larger indoor space. If students begin to complain that the game is not fair, say that you understand why they think this is the case and that they will be given an opportunity to discuss the game after it is over. Tell them that for now they should just go along with how the race is being run. If a student refuses to participate, do not force him or her to play.

When the game is over, discuss the questions on page 23 of the student journal as a class. To get the discussion started, talk about the students' reactions during the game. For example, point out if some students complained that the game wasn't fair, if some students didn't complain at all, or if other students refused to play such an unfair game. After the discussion, explain that in the next two classes the class will discuss how to respond when life is "unfair" in much more serious ways than in this game.

2. **Telling the Story** (10 minutes)

Students read the Twitter feed on pages 24–25 of the journal to themselves and write their own tweets or draw emojis. Encourage students to share their tweets with the group.

3. **Digging Deeper** (15 minutes)

Students answer the questions on page 26 in pairs. Possible answers include:

1) *Moses and Aaron may have been motivated by God instructing them to go to Pharaoh, and/or they may have had compassion for their people, who were enslaved.*
2) *Perhaps Moses and Aaron were realistic. They knew that Pharaoh would never free his slaves outright, but they thought he might consider allowing them to have a three-day break. If Pharaoh would agree to three days, the people of Israel could escape.*
3) *Pharaoh did not want to give his slaves even a short break; he wanted them to work for him all the time and not have even a taste of freedom. Also, we know from elsewhere in the story that God hardened Pharaoh's heart.*

As a class, discuss the first question, as well as the larger question: What motivates people to fight for justice? Is it a belief that God wants people to seek justice? Compassion for victims of injustice? Or some inner sense of what is right and wrong?

4. **Making Meaning** (10 minutes)

Write the word *tzedek* (צדק) on the board in Hebrew and define it for the class. Then have students answer the questions on page 27 on their own. If there is time, students can share ideas in small groups.

5. **Wrapping It Up: Try This!** (5 minutes)

Tell students to do the exercise on the bottom of page 29 of their student-response journals at home and to report back to the class at the next lesson. If there is time, ask students to begin brainstorming social-justice issues that their families are passionate about. Their families can add to the list later and think together about what they can do to promote those causes.

Extension Activity

SINGING TOGETHER (PAGE 27): Listen to the song "Go Down Moses" together. (A link to the song is available on the course website, www.behrmanhouse.com/values-bible.) Then discuss the question in this section of the student journal as a class. Possible answers include: *Slaves in the United States saw parallels between their experience and the experience of the Israelite slaves in Egypt. They found hope in the story of Moses and the Israelites' redemption from Egyptian slavery.*

Resources for the Teacher

For discussions about the history of the African American gospel song "Go Down Moses," see the course website at www.behrmanhouse.com/values-bible.

Chapter ❸ / Lesson 2

Essential Question: How can we work to make our communities more just?

Goals: In this lesson, students will:

1. Learn about Jewish people today who work to promote social justice.
2. Distinguish between the values of courage, leadership, and justice.
3. Identify ways that they can help fix injustices in their communities.

Lesson at a Glance

Many Jewish people today work to make our world more just, just as Moses and Aaron did in biblical times. In this lesson, students learn about people who promote social justice and reflect on how they can apply what they learned by acting to promote justice in their own communities.

Materials Needed

- Device with Internet access for each group
- Printouts of short biographies of each person featured in the Values in Action exercise, if Internet is not available to students in the classroom. (See Resources for the Teacher at the end of this lesson for where to find the printouts.)

Activities

1. Getting Started: Try This! (10 minutes)

Those students who wish to share with the class what social-justice causes their families are passionate about (the Wrapping It Up assignment from the previous lesson) report their findings to the class. Ask students to explain why these causes are important to them and their families.

2. Values in Action (15 minutes)

Students break into small groups for the activity on pages 28–29 of their journals. Assign each group a different person to research for this exercise. If the classroom has Internet access, ask students to research their person online. If the classroom has no Internet access, come to class with printouts describing these people's lives for the students to use (see Resources for the Teacher at the end of this lesson for information about where to find these printouts). When they are done researching/reading about their person, each group should write a few sentences in the voice of the person they researched that describes why that person was committed to his or her cause. Each group then reads what they wrote to the class.

3. Courage, Leadership, and Justice (10 minutes)

Do the exercise on pages 30–31 of the student-response journal as a class. You can use this exercise to summarize and review the three values the students have examined since the beginning of the course. Draw the Venn diagram on the board, and write students' answers inside the appropriate spaces. Use the completed diagram as a springboard for a deeper class discussion about how the values are interconnected. For example, ask: Why does it take courage to become a leader?

4. *Tzedek* and Me (10 minutes)

Ask the class to answer the questions on page 33 of their journals on their own. If there is time, they can share their answers in pairs.

5. Wrapping It Up: Community Project (5 minutes)

Have the students begin brainstorming ideas for community projects related to social justice. For each suggestion, ask students to think about what steps would be necessary for doing the project. Explain that the ideas for community projects that they think of now can likely be used for the community-project assignment later in the course.

Extension Activity

TORAH TIMELINE (PAGE 32): Students should do this exercise in pairs. Point out to the class that many different factors could have given Moses the strength to keep confronting Pharaoh, such as his belief in God, his dedication to the people of Israel, his dedication to the ideal of justice, or the support of his brother, Aaron. So too, each one of us can find our sources of strength to keep fighting for what we believe in.

Resources for the Teacher

For information on the people in the Values in Action exercise, visit the course website at www.behrmanhouse.com/values-bible.

Chapter 4

What Am I Thankful For? *Song of the Sea*

Lesson 1

Essential Question: How can Moses and Miriam's songs of thanks after the Israelites cross the Sea of Reeds inspire us to be thankful in our own lives?

Goals: In this lesson, students will:

1. Analyze the story of crossing the Sea of Reeds, focusing on Moses and Miriam's songs of thanks.
2. Define the word *hodayah* (thankfulness) and explain how Moses and Miriam expressed their thankfulness.
3. Explain how being thankful can help us and our communities.

Lesson at a Glance

After the Israelites crossed the Sea of Reeds to freedom, Moses and Miriam led the people in songs of thanks to God. In this lesson, students explore this biblical story through art, song, and a close reading of the original text. They also write thank-you notes to each other and discuss how thankfulness can make our communities stronger.

Materials Needed

- Markers
- Strips of paper
- Hat (or box)

Activities

1. Getting Started: Try This! (10 minutes)

Have the class do the first exercise on page 34 of the student journal. Prepare the strips of paper in advance, making one for each student. On one side of each strip, write a student's name. On the other side of the strip, write: "Thank you for . . . " When class begins, fold up the strips of paper, put them in a hat (or box), and ask each student to pick a name from the hat. Students should write a thank-you note to the person whose name they picked and then hand them in (without signing their names). After all the notes have been handed in, give each student the thank-you note written for him or her. (Before giving the notes out, read through them to make sure they are written appropriately.) When they are done reading their thank-you notes, students complete the sentences on page 34 of their journals.

As a class, discuss: How did this exercise make me feel about my classroom community?

Explain that in this lesson the class will discuss why saying thank you is important and how it can help strengthen our communities.

2. **Telling the Story** (15 minutes)

Students do this exercise (pages 35–36 in their journals) individually and then share their illustrations in pairs.

3. **Digging Deeper** (10 minutes)

Working with the same partner as the last exercise, students answer the questions on page 37.

Possible answers to the questions are below. Discuss the second question as a class.

1) *They were thankful to God for delivering them from the Egyptians.*
2) *Although the Israelites were presumably thankful to God when they left Egypt, when they received the Torah, and at many other moments in the Exodus story, this moment marked the transition between slavery and freedom, when at last they no longer needed to fear the Egyptians. Before they crossed the Sea of Reeds, the Israelites feared for their lives as they saw the army of the Egyptians, who had been their masters, advance toward them. Then God miraculously delivered them to freedom, and so they thanked God.*
3) *The song of Miriam and the women was unique. It was expressed in a different way and involved different voices than Moses's song. We see from Miriam's song that every member of the people of Israel was included in singing and expressing their thankfulness.*

4. **Making Meaning** (10 minutes)

Write the word *hodayah* (הודיה) on the board in Hebrew and define it as a class. Then discuss the questions on page 38 of the student journal as a class. Remind students of their discussion at the beginning of the lesson about how writing and receiving thank-you notes made them feel about their classroom community.

5. **Wrapping It Up: Singing Together** (5 minutes)

Listen to Debbie Friedman's "Miriam's Song" together. A link to the song is available at the course website, www.behrmanhouse.com/values-bible. Discuss the question about the song on page 38 of the student-response journal together. Why was it important for the Torah to specify that the women not only sang, but also played musical instruments and danced?

Resources for the Teacher

For more on the importance of being thankful and how being thankful can help people feel happier and lower their stress levels, see www.behrmanhouse.com/values-bible.

Chapter ❹ / Lesson 2

Essential Question: What are the challenges to being thankful and what helps us be more thankful?

Goals: In this lesson, students will:

1. Express what they are thankful for in their own lives.
2. Debate whether one should be thankful for something that causes others to suffer.
3. Identify what helps them be thankful for things in their lives and what makes it difficult.

Lesson at a Glance

On the one hand, Jewish tradition encourages us to be thankful and provides many opportunities for us to express our thanks. On the other hand, our tradition acknowledges the challenges of being thankful. In this lesson, students look at the traditional prayer of thanks that Jews recite in the morning and write their own thank-you prayers, poems, or songs. Students then read a midrash in which God admonishes the angels for singing a song of thanks at the Sea of Reeds while God's creatures were dying. This midrash, together with the manna story in Exodus, is used as a springboard for exploring what makes being thankful more difficult and what helps us to be thankful.

Materials Needed

- Construction paper
- Markers

Activities

1. Getting Started: ***Modeh/Modah Ani*** (10 minutes)

Read *"Modeh/Modah Ani"* (page 39 of the student journal) together as a class, and ask the students to say the prayer in their own words. (For example: *"Thank you, God, for giving me life each and every morning."*) Discuss the first question on page 39 as a class. Remind students of their discussion during the last lesson about why thankfulness is important.

Students then write their own song, poem, or prayer individually, on page 39. Those who wish to can share a line or more from what they wrote and/or what they felt while writing it.

If there is time, students can write their song, poem, or prayer on a colorful piece of paper and decorate it (without writing their names). If possible, hang the papers in the classroom.

2. Rabbis' Corner (15 minutes)

In pairs, students read the midrash on page 40 and answer the questions. Possible answers include:

1) *God felt that the angels should have had compassion for the Egyptians, because no matter how evil they were, they too were God's creations.*

2) *Perhaps the Israelites could not be held to the same standards as the angels. The Israelites were human, and it is human to celebrate being saved from your enemies, even if that means that your enemies died as a result.*
3) *On the one hand, the Israelites should thank God for saving their lives, and one could argue that the Egyptians deserved their punishment. On the other hand, they shouldn't celebrate anyone's death.*
4) *We should be thankful for our blessings from God; however, we shouldn't thank God for others' suffering. Nevertheless, it is often the case that my blessings can cause others to suffer.*
   Some examples from the students' lives include: *If I am elected class president, one of my classmates will lose the election. I make the softball team, but my friend does not.*

Students debate the third question as a class. They can use parallel examples from their lives or current events to make their arguments, and they can also cite the rabbis or the biblical text itself. Make sure that students present both sides of the debate (even if it is not the side they believe in). The class can then vote on the answer to the debate question.

3. **Torah Timeline** (10 minutes)

Students do this exercise (page 41) in small groups. Go around to each group to make sure they are on task and understand the story. Encourage students to think more deeply about the questions by putting themselves in the Israelites' shoes. Remind them that even though slavery in Egypt was horrible, it was all they knew, and the unknown is scary. Sometimes it is hard to be thankful about being forced to leave what you know and do something new, even if the new thing might ultimately be a blessing.

4. ***Hodayah* and Me** (10 minutes)

Students do the exercise on page 42 of their journals individually. Encourage students to actually go out and thank the person they write about. Ask students to share what they wrote in the chart with the class, and make a chart on the board including different students' answers. Remind the class to draw on what they discussed in Torah Timeline about the reason the Israelites had difficulty being thankful.

5. **Wrapping It Up: Try This!** (5 minutes)

Ask students to brainstorm about people in their community whom they would like to thank (as described on page 42 of the student journal), and to consider how they would like to thank them. If there is time, students can work on a short project, such as writing thank-you cards for someone, as part of this lesson. If they think of a larger project related to *hodayah*, they can choose to do it as their community project.

Extension Activity

A HUNDRED BLESSINGS: There is a Jewish tradition to say a hundred blessings each day, thanking God for specific gifts in our lives as we go through the day. (Visit the course website, www.behrmanhouse.com/values-bible, to learn more about this tradition.) In small groups, students should make a list of all the things they would say a blessing for each day. Tell them to be as specific as possible (i.e. do not just list "food," but the different kinds of food they eat each day). Point out that some of the blessings can be easily overlooked, such as the blessing said after going to the bathroom. Students should see if they can get to a hundred blessings.

For a calculation of how the rabbis reached this number of blessings, see the course website, www.behrmanhouse.com/values-bible.

Resources for the Teacher

For background information on the Talmud, more insights into the questions raised in the Rabbis' Corner exercise, and more on how we can practice gratitude in our daily lives, visit www.behrmanhouse.com/values-bible.

Chapter 5

What Am I Committed To? *Receiving the Torah*

Lesson 1

Essential Question: How can the Israelites receiving the Torah on Mount Sinai inspire us to make and keep our commitments?

Goals: In this lesson, students will:

1. Look closely at God's Covenant with the people of Israel at Mount Sinai.
2. Provide interpretations of what it means for the people of Israel to be a "treasured people."
3. Define the word *brit* (covenant) and explain why it was important in making the Jewish people into a nation.

Lesson at a Glance

At Mount Sinai, God and the Jewish people made a covenant (a set of mutual commitments) with one another. In this lesson, students examine those commitments closely and begin to think about the role that commitment plays in their own lives and communities.

Materials Needed

- Markers
- Ball

Activities

1. Getting Started: Get on the Move (10 minutes)

Clear a large open area in the classroom so that students can form a large circle and have room to throw a ball. An inflatable beach ball may be easiest to use in the classroom. Play the game on page 43 of the journal together as a class.

Students should then answer the questions individually. A few students may share with the class why the commitment they chose is important to them.

2. Telling the Story (15 minutes)

Act out the story on page 44 as a class. You can have the student playing Moses climb on top of a chair to act out being on top of Mount Sinai, and then climb down from the chair to act out talking to the people.

When the students are finished acting out the story, assign some students to act as journalists and other students to pretend to be Israelites. The journalist students should think of questions they would like to ask the Israelites and write them down on page 44 of their journals. Then they can ask them of their classmates who are acting as Israelites. Their classmates answer as they imagine an Israelite at Mount Sinai might have answered.

3. **Digging Deeper** (15 minutes)

Write the contract that is written on page 45 of the student-response journal on the board, and fill in the blanks as a class. The completed contract could look something like this:

If you listen to Me and keep my Covenant, I commit to making you my special people and a holy nation. Signed, God	I commit to do everything that God says. Signed, The People of Israel

Students answer the rest of the questions on page 45 in pairs. Possible answers include:

1) *I have a special necklace that I got from my grandmother. I wear it all the time, and if I need to take it off, I am very careful to put it someplace safe, where I will not lose it.*
2) *God has a special relationship with the people of Israel. God wants to always be close to them. God is committed to the people of Israel and looks out for them.*
3) *They are promising to listen to whatever God says, even though they do not know yet what God will ask them to do.*
4) *Perhaps the people of Israel committed themselves to keeping God's Covenant because they were grateful to God for taking them out of Egypt. Maybe they were looking for laws and beliefs to define themselves as a people now that they had left Egypt.*

Discuss the second question as a class. This passage raises difficult questions regarding the Jewish people's chosenness. Are the Jews God's chosen people? If so, what does that mean? Does it imply that Jews are better than other people, or does it mean something else?

Make sure to point out that this passage does not say anything about the Jews being "chosen"; it says that the Jewish people are treasured and holy. The phrase "the chosen people," in fact, does not appear in the Bible. Being God's treasured people indicates there is a close relationship between God and the people of Israel, which, as we have seen, brings mutual commitment and responsibility. Being God's treasured people does not mean that we are better than others, but that we have a special task in this world.

See the Resources for the Teacher section at the end of this lesson for links to more insights into the concept of chosenness, the question of what it means to be "a kingdom of priests and a holy people," and how the Israelites committed to keeping God's Covenant before they knew what it would be.

4. Wrapping It Up: Making Meaning (10 minutes)

Write the word *brit* (ברית) on the board and define it as a class. Discuss the first two questions on page 46 in the student-response journal. Possible answers include:

1) *A covenant is an agreement between at least two parties in which each party makes promises or commitments to the other. The Covenant between God and the Jewish people helped the Jews become a nation by giving them a common set of laws and beliefs that unites them as a people.*
2) *Commitment between people unites a community and helps it function smoothly. For example, the people of a certain community may commit to not lying to or hurting one another, to taking care of the poor or sick within the community, or to working together to make the world a more just place.*

Each student now draws the picture at the bottom of page 46. If there is time, students share their pictures in small groups.

Resources for the Teacher

See the course website, www.behrmanhouse.com/values-bible, for:

- Insights into what it means for the Jews to be God's chosen people.
- An explanation of what it means to be "a kingdom of priests and a holy nation."
- A discussion of why the Israelites said "We will do" before they knew what it was that they were committing to. The Israelites' promise is related to their assertion later on at Mount Sinai that, "We will do and we will hear" (*na'aseh ve-nishma*), which could also be translated as "We will do and we will understand." The Israelites are also committing to understanding what they are doing, even if their actions are not dependent on understanding first.

Chapter 5 / Lesson 2

Essential Question: What commitments are important to me personally and to us as a community?

Goals: In this lesson, students will:

1. Make their own classroom covenant, outlining their commitments to each other as a classroom community.
2. Discuss the relevance of the Covenant at Sinai and the Ten Commandments today.
3. Identify commitments that they have in their own lives.

Lesson at a Glance

According to the rabbis, every Jew from every generation received the Torah at Mount Sinai. What does that mean for Jewish people today? What does the idea of covenant, and particularly the Covenant at Mount Sinai, have to do with each one of us? In this lesson, students reflect on commitments they have made in their own lives, namely the commitments they have made to their classmates and families, their ancestors, the Torah, and themselves. To better understand the importance of covenant, students make their own classroom covenant, outlining their commitments to one another.

Materials Needed

- A large poster board
- Markers

Activities

1. Getting Started: Rabbis' Corner (8 minutes)

Students respond to the prompts on page 47 of their journals individually. Ask a few students to share their responses to one of the prompts, making sure that different students share responses to each of the three prompts.

2. Class Covenant (20 minutes)

Complete the exercise on page 48 of the student journal as a class. Before beginning, remind students that comments that are hurtful to others will not be tolerated and that hurtful comments break down the classroom community rather than make it better. Explain that as the teacher, you retain veto power if suggestions are made that you feel are hurtful or mean-spirited.

As a class, brainstorm ways the students would like to see their classroom community improve. For example, students might suggest listening more closely to each other or making everyone in the class feel included. Then ask students to suggest specific commitments that can help the classroom community improve, such as: "I will not talk when another person is talking" or "If I see someone alone or left out, I will invite them to join me and my friends."

After each commitment is suggested, students vote on the commitment by a show of hands. Write the approved commitments on the board. Encourage students to make the commitments as specific as possible.

When the class finishes defining the commitments, ask one student with neat handwriting to write the final list of commitments on a poster board, and have each student sign his or her name. Other students can decorate the poster. When it is finished, hang up the poster in the classroom. Tell the class that if they see students breaking one of the commitments, they can point to the poster to remind the student(s) of their commitments.

3. **Torah Timeline** (10 minutes)

Students discuss the questions on page 49 of their journals in pairs. Before the class breaks into pairs, remind students that this classroom is a safe space and each person should listen to their partner express what he or she is committed to without being judgmental. If students want to clarify what their partner thinks, they can ask their partner some questions in order to understand them better (such as "Why do you feel committed to that?" rather than, "How could you believe in that?!"). Tell students to refrain from responding positively or negatively to what is said.

If there is time, discuss as a class how the Covenant with God helped the people of Israel establish themselves as a community. Possible answers include:

- *These commandments gave the people of Israel beliefs and values that united them.*
- *These commandments helped prevent the people from hurting one another and enabled them to live together peacefully.*

4. ***Brit* and Me** (7 minutes)

Each person completes this exercise (on page 50 of the journal) individually.

As a class, discuss what helps, and what makes it hard, for the students to keep their commitments. If there is time, ask for volunteers to share one of the commitments that they wrote.

5. **Wrapping It Up: Try This!** (5 minutes)

Introduce the exercise at the bottom of page 48 for the students to do at home. To get them started, have them write (in class) one example of a commitment they would like to include in their family covenant. Students can share their family covenants at the beginning of the next lesson if they want to.

Resources for the Teacher

See the course website, www.behrmanhouse.com/values-bible, for an interpretation of the Ten Commandments as statements rather than commandments; interpretations of the relevance of the Ten Commandments today; and several possible divisions of the Ten Commandments.

Chapter 6

How Can I Learn to Forgive? *The Golden Calf*

Lesson 1

Essential Question: How can the story of the Golden Calf help us learn to forgive?

Goals: In this lesson, students will:

1. Analyze the story of the Golden Calf.
2. Define *s'lichah* (forgiveness) and discuss how Moses and God demonstrate forgiveness.
3. Identify the benefits of forgiveness for the forgiver, the forgiven, and the community.

Lesson at a Glance

Right after God and the Israelites made their Covenant at Mount Sinai, the Israelites broke the Covenant by making the Golden Calf. Despite this grave sin, Moses prayed to God to forgive the people, and God granted the people forgiveness. In this lesson, students explore why Moses and God chose to forgive the people even though what the people did was clearly wrong. Through examining this biblical story students consider the benefits and limits of forgiveness.

Activities

1. Getting Started: What Would You Do? (15 minutes)

Divide students into groups of four for the exercise on page 51 of the student-response journal. In each group, each student takes a part as Abby, Sarah, themselves, or the narrator of the story. Have half the groups act out what would happen if they chose to forgive Sarah after she asked for forgiveness several times, and ask the other half of the groups to act out what would happen if they would not forgive her. Give each group five minutes to talk about the scenario and to practice acting it out. Encourage students to imagine not only what would happen immediately, but also in a few days or a few months. Ask them: How would what happened affect your relationship with Sarah in the long term? Will you ever be as close friends as you were before? What might happen if Abby makes fun of you in front of Sarah again? How will she, and you, respond?

Gather the groups together. Choose one group to act out for the class what might happen if they forgive Sarah and one group to act out what might happen if they don't. Invite the other groups to say how they think things might happen differently. Then have a class vote on what they would do. Ask students to defend each choice.

2. Telling the Story (10 minutes)

Students read the text on page 52 and write the blog entries on pages 52–53 individually. As a class, discuss: Do you think Moses should have asked God to forgive the people of Israel? Why or why not?

3. **Digging Deeper** (15 minutes)

Students answer the questions on page 54 of their journals in pairs. Possible answers include:

1) *Moses and God are committed to the people of Israel and the Covenant between the people of Israel and God. This commitment to the relationship enables them to forgive the people of Israel even when they did something very wrong. Perhaps God and Moses also understand that because the people of Israel were slaves for so many years, they are still learning how to be responsible for their actions and make ethical choices.*
2) *Just because God forgives the people does not mean that the people of Israel do not have to face the consequences of their actions; God still punishes them with a plague. So too, just because Moses forgives the people does not mean he was not angry at them for what they did. Forgiveness in this situation allows the relationship between God, Moses, and the Jewish people to continue, and God does not abandon the Jewish people.*
3) *Asking forgiveness of God becomes an important part of the Jewish people's relationship with God and, therefore, their prayers. An important part of being Jewish is recognizing when we do something wrong, asking forgiveness, and resolving not to do the wrong thing again.*

Discuss the second question as a class. It is important that students understand that forgiveness does not mean that everyone pretends that something never happened. Even when there is forgiveness, there are still consequences for our actions.

4. **Wrapping It Up: Making Meaning** (10 minutes)

Define *s'lichah* and discuss the questions on page 55 as a class. Stress that every committed, healthy relationship requires forgiveness.

Resources for the Teacher

For insights on how forgiveness can benefit the person who forgives, see the course website at www.behrmanhouse.com/values-bible.

Chapter 6 / Lesson 2

Essential Question: How can forgiveness build community?

Goals: In this lesson, students will:

1. Discuss a rabbinic text on the obligation to forgive.
2. Debate the limits of forgiveness.
3. Identify challenges to forgiveness and how they can be overcome.

Lesson at a Glance

If God and Moses could forgive the people of Israel after the Golden Calf, does that mean that anyone can be forgiven? Or are there people who have committed such evil acts that no matter how many times they beg for forgiveness, they should not be forgiven? In this lesson, students explore these questions by studying a text from Maimonides on the obligation to forgive and staging a mock trial of Oskar Groening, the bookkeeper of Auschwitz.

Materials Needed

- Markers

Activities

1. **Getting Started: Forgiveness and Community** (10 minutes)

Students do the drawing exercise on page 56 of their journals individually. When they are finished, discuss the question at the bottom of page 56 as a class. Ask the students to base their comments on the pictures they drew. They can show their pictures to the class to demonstrate a particular advantage or disadvantage in a society. Make sure to come up with both advantages and disadvantages for both kinds of societies.

2. **Rabbis' Corner** (10 minutes)

Students should do this exercise (page 57 of the journal) in pairs. Discuss the last question as a class. Connect the text to the scene the students acted out during the last lesson in the What Would You Do? section. Ask the students: What would Maimonides have said about this situation? Do you agree? Why or why not?

3. **Mock Trial** (20 minutes)

For the activity on page 58 (a mock trial of Oskar Groening), divide the students into two groups—prosecution and defense. The prosecution and defense both take a few minutes to prepare short arguments (one to two minutes) to present to the teacher, who will act as judge.

After the groups prepare on their own, they come together for the trial. The defense and prosecution each present their arguments, and then the judge can ask more questions. The defense and prosecution answer.

Each student then answers the questions on page 58 in the student journal. They should answer what they themselves think, independent of whether they were assigned to the prosecution or defense group. After they have written down their position, discuss as a class how and why they made their decision.

4. Wrapping It Up: *S'lichah* and Me (10 minutes)

Students answer the questions on page 59 individually. If there is time, they can share their answers in pairs.

Extension Activities

TRY THIS! (Page 59): Students may do this exercise at home, with their families, or together with the class. Ideas of reminders could include: "No one is perfect"; "Everyone makes mistakes"; "Forgive yourself"; or "Forgiveness is not for others, it's for yourself."

FORGIVENESS AROUND THE WORLD: Have students research how different countries have addressed questions of forgiveness and reconciliation on a national level following violent internal conflict. How do two peoples who were once enemies live together peacefully? Can one forgive someone who attacked, killed, or otherwise hurt one's family members? What happens when violence is so widespread that punishing everyone involved would mean punishing a significant part of the population? Examples include Rwanda following the 1994 genocide or South Africa following apartheid. See the course website for more information about these two examples.

Resources for the Teacher

The course website, www.behrmanhouse.com/values-bible, offers additional resources, including more information about Maimonides; a discussion of whether, according to the Torah, some people should not be forgiven; the case of Oskar Groening and how one Auschwitz survivor embraced and forgave him.

Chapter 7

What Can I Give? *Building the Tabernacle*

Lesson 1

Essential Question: How can the story of building the Tabernacle inspire me to give?

Goals: In this lesson, students will:

1. Look closely at the biblical story of building the Tabernacle.
2. Define *n'tinah* (giving) and explain how the Israelites demonstrated this quality when building the Tabernacle.
3. Discuss the importance of each person making a unique contribution to the community.

Lesson at a Glance

The Torah describes in great detail the many different things that the Israelites contributed to the building of the Tabernacle. In this lesson, students look closely at the language used by the Bible to describe the building of the Tabernacle, and they make their own models of the Tabernacle in small groups. Through group work, students explore the importance of each person making his or her unique contribution to the community.

Materials Needed

- Building blocks, Legos, pieces of fabric, pipe cleaners, shoe boxes, or any other materials that might be useful for building the model Tabernacle
- Camera
- Printer

Activities

1. Getting Started: Get on the Move, Part I (5 minutes)

Explain the gift-exchange game to students (on page 60 of the journal), and give each student the name of the person they will be giving gifts to during the coming week.

2. Telling the Story (25 minutes)

Read the passage from Exodus on page 61 together, and have students explain the passage in their own words. Divide the students into small groups to build models of the Tabernacle.

When the groups complete their models, students should walk around the room quietly to look at all the models. Have one person from each group stand beside the model to answer questions. If there is time, a representative from each group can present its model to the class and explain why the group made it in that specific way.

Students should photograph their group's model Tabernacle, print out the photo, and paste it to page 62 of their journals. If there is no printer in the classroom, make a sketch of the model instead. Then each student answers the questions on page 62 individually.

Discuss: What would have happened if all my classmates had contributed the same thing to making the model?

3. **Digging Deeper** (10 minutes)

Students answer the questions on page 63 of their journals in pairs. Possible answers include:

1) *The Torah describes the many different gifts in detail to emphasize how each person contributed something unique to building the Tabernacle.*
2) *These words let us know that each person gave voluntarily to the building of the Tabernacle. No one was forced to contribute; these were gifts from the heart. The Torah acknowledges how the contributions were made so that we can learn lessons about giving.*

As a class, discuss what students can learn about the Israelites contributing to the building of the Tabernacle by using their own experiences of building a model Tabernacle with others. What would have happened if all of the Israelites had given the same thing to the Tabernacle? Why was it so important that everyone gave different things, just as in the group project?

4. **Wrapping It Up: Making Meaning** (10 minutes)

Define the word *n'tinah,* and discuss the questions on page 64 of the journal as a class.

Extension Activity

COMPARISON TO THE GOLDEN CALF: Look closely at the verses describing the building of the Golden Calf (Exodus 32:1–4). Compare and contrast this passage to the description of building the Tabernacle. How was the manner in which the Israelites gave different in each situation?
A possible answer is: *For the Golden Calf, each person contributed the same thing, whereas during the building of the Tabernacle, each person offered something different. Part of the greatness of the Tabernacle was that it was made up of unique, individual contributions, whereas the Golden Calf was the result of conformity.*

Resources for the Teacher

For more on the benefits of giving, see the course website, www.behrmanhouse.com/values-bible.

Chapter ❼ / Lesson 2

Essential Question: How does giving build community?

Goals: In this lesson, students will:

1. Give examples of when giving conflicts with focusing on oneself and discuss how to deal with such situations.
2. Recognize different students' contributions to their classroom community.
3. Review the values from earlier chapters and explain how acting upon each value can help them to give to their communities.

Lesson at a Glance

Each community requires the unique gifts of many people in order to function. In this lesson, students find out more about the different people who give to their community by interviewing various people who work, or help in some way, in their school. Students also explore how they can give to their communities and what happens when giving to others conflicts with one's own self-interest.

Activities

1. Getting Started: Get on the Move, Part II (10 minutes)

After a week of playing the gift-exchange game in which students give secretly to the person whose name they were assigned (see page 60 in the student journal), students reveal who was giving to whom. Students should then respond to the prompts on page 60 individually. Discuss the last prompt as a class.

2. What Would You Do? (10 minutes)

In pairs, students act out the conversation between themselves and a friend that might take place in the scenario described on page 64 of their journals. Students should respond as they think they would have responded to the request to make brownies. Partners should then switch roles so that the other person in the pair has a chance to act out how he or she would have responded in this situation.

Ask students to respond to the prompts on page 64 individually. Then, discuss the questions as a class. Ask students to bring other examples from their lives of situations when giving to others has come into conflict with focusing on themselves, and discuss how they made decisions in this kind of situation. Make sure to emphasize that everyone has to draw a line somewhere by saying "I can give this but not that" and that saying no to requests for help is a natural and necessary part of life.

3. Values in Action (20 minutes)

Break the students into small groups for the activity on pages 65–66, and assign each group one person to interview. You can use the suggestions of people to interview that are provided in the student journal, or you can choose other contributors who are more relevant to your school community. If necessary, students can call the person on the phone.

Groups should begin their interviews by thanking the person they are interviewing for his or her contributions. Then they should ask about what motivates that person to contribute to the school; what the challenges are in making this contribution; and how the person overcomes these challenges. Each group writes down the answers to the questions and reports back to the class.

If possible, notify the contributors ahead of time that students will be coming to interview them, and make sure that they are comfortable speaking to the students for a few minutes. If interviewing is not feasible in your school, ask each group to imagine how the person would respond and to write the answer in that person's voice.

After presenting their interviews to the class, students should respond to the prompts on page 66 of their journals individually.

4. Wrapping It Up: *N'tinah* and Me (10 minutes)

Students respond to the prompts on page 67 individually. Invite students to share one of their answers with the class.

Extension Activity

TRY THIS! (PAGE 67): Ask students to do this activity at home with their families. In order to get them started in class, have students write down one way they already contribute to their families and one new way that they would like to contribute to their families in the future.

My Community Project

Introducing the Project

This project is introduced to the students in the first chapter of the student-response journal, and students brainstorm together for project ideas throughout the course. You may choose to set aside class periods (or half-periods) to work on the community project throughout the second half of the course, after chapter 4. Alternatively, you can give the class several consecutive days to complete the project at the end of the course.

Students may choose to work on the project individually, in pairs, or in small groups.

Step #1: Identify Your Community's Needs and Your Resources

Timing: half-period

Prior to this lesson, students interview different people in the community about what they think are the community's needs. In class, students brainstorm about the needs of the community. Instruct the class to make sure that they phrase the problem as a need that has not yet been met. Examples could include:

- *Students in our school need to be protected from bullying.*
- *Overworked staff members at our school need to be appreciated.*
- *Our synagogue needs Braille prayer books.*
- *Some schools in our city need books and computers.*
- *Young students at the local elementary school need help learning to read.*
- *Elderly people in the apartment building next to our school need companionship.*

Students should also discuss their personal skills, talents, or interests that they can use to contribute to the community. To get students thinking about their unique abilities, begin a discussion about different talents, and then have students write on page 68 in their journals individually.

Examples could include:

- *Working with younger children.*
- *Making posters that get people's attention.*
- *Coordinating lots of different people to help them work together.*
- *Accompanying elderly people.*
- *Spreading messages on social media.*

Step #2: Choose a Project

Timing: half-period

Students use this time to choose a project. If they wish to collaborate with other students, they may form pairs or groups to work on their projects. Tell the class that they must get approval of their project from you before beginning their work.

Students fill out the prompts on page 69 of their journals individually.

Step #3: Plan Your Project

Timing: half-period

Students fill out the chart on page 70 in the student journal, outlining the steps needed to do the community project. Those who are working on their own should share their chart with a partner to receive feedback. All charts should be approved by you.

When you review the charts, make sure that students have remembered to include the steps needed to gather information before beginning the actual work on the project. For example, if a project involves tutoring younger children at the local elementary school in reading, the student would first need to meet with the children's teacher(s) to learn more about the specific children and what kind of help they need. The student should also read material about teaching children to read.

Step #4: Do Your Project

Timing: two periods, plus time at home (or more time during school, if necessary)

Students complete their projects with your close guidance. When students have completed their projects, they respond to the prompts on page 71 in the student journal individually.

Give students the opportunity to let others know about their project by having them make a poster or give a brief talk about the results of their project (two to five minutes per project). They may want to include testimony from people they helped, the amount of money they raised, or photos of them doing the project. They can also discuss their responses to the prompts in the student journal.

If possible, host a special event at your school for the student presentations. Invite students' families or other classes to attend. At the event, students present their projects and receive feedback. If this is not possible, they can present their projects to each other in class and receive feedback from the other students.

Glossary

Brit — covenant and commitment

G'vurah — courage

Hodayah — thankfulness

Manhigut — leadership

Midah —character trait

Midrash — rabbinic interpretation of biblical text

Mishkan — the Tabernacle

Mitzvot — commandments

Modeh/Modah Ani — a short prayer traditionally said upon waking; literally, "I thank."

N'tinah — giving

S'lichah — forgiveness

Tzedek — justice